Spices

Written by Rob Alcraft

KUDOS

Published by Kudos, an imprint of Top That! Publishing plc.
Copyright © 2004 Top That! Publishing plc,
Tide Mill Way, Woodbridge, Suffolk, IP12 IAP.
www.kudosbooks.com

Kudos is a Trademark of Top That! Publishing plc

CONTENTS

INTRODUCTION

The aroma of spices has been appreciated since earliest civilisation. It is a scent from the ancient bazaars of the East, and the trailing caravans of the Arabian Desert. It is a scent from the tombs of the ancient Egyptians, who used spices to embalm the dead, and to sustain them in the afterlife. It is a scent of the ancient cultures of Greece and Rome, who valued some spices more than gold, and believed that they came from the edge of the world, where the seas boiled.

Today spices still conjure a taste of the exotic – but they are cheaper and more widely available than ever before. Cooks across the world can flavour food with spices once so precious they were considered the preserve of the gods. This book attempts to tell the story of spices, how they came to us, and at what cost. It looks at uses, tradition, flavours, and how to tell good from bad. Knowing about spices frees even experienced cooks to enjoy them more, and to use them with confidence, transforming food and drink with flavours ancient and new.

DEFINING SPICES

Spices have been used, and traded, since earliest history. Part food, part drug, spices have always been valued for their flavour, as preservatives, for their perfume, and for their aromatic and medicinal power.

Spices include a huge variety of plants – and plant parts. In this sense they are difficult to define, for they are buds and flowers, both fresh and dried. They are seeds and fruits, roots, bark, sap, gum and leaves. They are used as powders, they are crushed, grated, bruised and chewed. They are cooked and dried, and steeped and burnt.

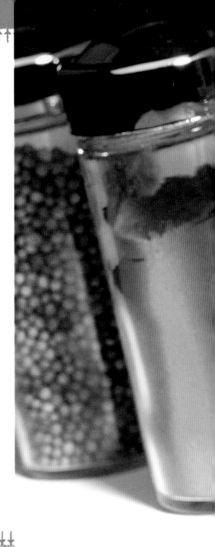

THE RAREST OF THINGS

Spices have always partly been defined by their rarity and value. For thousands of years, spices such as cloves were known only on a few islands in what is now Indonesia. Frankincense was obtainable only from one species of tree, in one distant desert country, on the far southern tip of the Arabian Desert.

Some spices were so rare that they are now extinct, such as silphium, a favourite flavour in ancient Greece and Rome. The last stem of this almost legendary plant was consumed by Emperor Nero, and today we can only guess at its taste.

LUXURY AND NECESSITY

In many cases spices are defined by the cultures that use them. Cinnamon, for example, was used by the Egyptians to embalm the dead, but it is now valued in pastries and pasta. What was a drug and preservative in one culture, can be a flavouring in another.

THE IMPORTANCE OF SPICES

Ever since the first trade routes opened between East and West, spices have had a dramatic influence on our world. It was the quest for spices that drove adventurers – often risking everything they had – from Europe, Arabia, China and India out across the world. They searched for trade routes that would give their merchant nation the edge over rivals.

When the first Arab and Greek mariners crossed the Indian Ocean to the Malabar coast of India, it was the rarity and value of spices that drove them. Later, it was the desire to trade spices that led Vasco da Gama to find a sea route south of the African continent. It was spices that drove explorers like Magellan and Columbus to risk everything in journeys that many of their contemporaries believed would pitch them from the edge of the world.

WEALTH AND CULTURE

The riches of the spice trade helped establish and build the intellectual cultures that have shaped modern civilisations and influenced the way in which we think about the world. From the trade in spices was born the intellectual and cultural strength of Venice and other city states of Italy such as Genoa and Florence. Spices enabled the great cities of Lisbon and Alexandria to prosper. The spice trade

aided the spread of Islam, which travelled east and west with the merchants of Arabia.

EMPIRE AND SLAVERY

The fabulous riches offered by the spice trade drove the first wave of conquest from Europe. The Dutch, Spanish and French all vied to conquer and control the sources of spices. The British Empire began with the conquest of the tiny Spice Island of Run, taken in 1602.

It can be argued that spices have cast a long shadow over the world's history. There is no doubt that the quest for spices has had an influence upon the great population movements, the beginnings of slavery and the destruction and mixing of cultures that has characterised the last 500 years.

SOURCES OF SPICES

For many millennia spices were attributed mysterious and legendary origins. Their arrival in the distant markets of the ancient world must have seemed as amazing as receiving plants from space. Early traders used this heady mix of ignorance and exoticism to increase the demand and value of their cargoes. They told extraordinary tales of journeys to boiling seas and lands of monsters. These stories still survive, for example in the story of cinnamon.

THE STORY OF CINNAMON

In the earliest surviving Greek prose book, *Herodotus' Histories* (*c.* 440 BC) he writes: 'The Arabians say that the dry sticks, which we call kinamomon, are brought to Arabia by large birds, which carry them to their nests, made of mud, on mountain precipices which no man can climb.'

Only when the Arabs induced the birds to overload their nests by spreading out the carcasses of slaughtered animals as bait, could the falling nests and the cinnamon be collected.

LUXURIES FROM THE EAST AND WEST

Many of the world's most valued and widely used spices originated in Asia and the Middle East. The word 'spice' comes from the Latin 'species', which meant literally any traded commodity, but came to refer to the exotic incense and flavours that originated in the East.

Some spices, such as ginger, were already widespread in tropical Asia by ancient times, having been transported by migrants and traders from southern China. Other spices, including some of the earliest known and most valuable, such as cloves, nutmeg, mace and cinnamon, grew only on a particular group of islands that came to be known as the Spice Islands – now the Moluccas in Indonesia.

In the sixteenth century, with the opening up of the Americas, there was an extraordinary and rapid exchange of spices between old world and new, East and West. Spices, such as ginger, chilli, sugar, vanilla and nutmeg, crossed the world in a giant leap of replanting, exchange and commerce. It is something of a twist and certainly unusual historically that, despite the West's rapacious interest, most of the world's commercial spices are still supplied from the East – today India is one of the world's biggest spice producers.

SPICES AS MEDICINES

Spices have been used in medicines, balms and ointments for thousands of years. Many are still part of the modern Western pharmacopeia – from cloves used in toothpastes and mouthwashes to camphor and aniseed used in cough mixtures, antiseptics, perfumes and soaps.

Hippocrates assembled a list of spices for remedial use in 400 BC. It is the first comprehensive study we have, but the usefulness of spices in Greek and world cultures had been known long before.

FRESH BREATH – AND POISON

Spices such as storax – a sweet-scented tree gum that originated in Syria – were considered by the Roman writer Pliny to be effective against melancholy. Another tree resin, mastic, was important for thousands of years as a medicine, and is still used as a breath-freshening gum in Greece and Turkey today.

Spices were also widely believed to be effective against poison and in generally restoring health. King Mathridates, who ruled in northeast Turkey in the first century BC, took a daily dose of around two dozen spices

as an antidote to poisons he expected to be fed by his enemies. The Romans also believed that many spices could act against poison, using them to treat anything from snakebites to scorpion stings.

BODY AND MIND

In ancient China, Rome and Arabia, and even in medieval Europe, it was thought that spices contributed to the body's natural balance and could be used to alter it. Spices such as ginger were hot, others, such as camphor were cold, and were used to heat or cool the body as appropriate.

Spices were often added to food for medical reasons, for example spikenard – the oil from the leaves and root of a Himalayan plant.

A surviving Roman recipe shows that spikenard was added to a hare dish for a diner suffering from dysentery.

SPICES FOR FLATULENCE AND PHLEGM

Early writers recommended a spice cure for virtually every ailment. There were spices for treating colds and colic, for cholera, and cloves for the eyes. Spices were used to treat flatulence, to exorcise spirits, to fumigate rooms and treat infertility and sores. Annatto was used as a sun cream in the Caribbean. Sandalwood was used in the same way in parts of Asia. Spices were used as digestives and soporifics, while long pepper was believed to regulate phlegm, act as a sexual stimulant and be effective in reviving a suffocated patient.

SPICES AS COSMETICS

Spices have always been valued for their perfume and aroma. The ancient Egyptians, enthusiastic about spices in food, also valued them as cosmetics and incense. Such spices were so prized that chroniclers of the time recorded that workers in the perfume factories had seals placed on their loincloths to prevent them from stealing even the tiniest fraction of the spices they worked with.

Tomb paintings from ancient Egypt show musicians at festivals wearing spice-filled cones in their hair, while there is evidence that skin oils and perfumes were considered so important that tomb workers who worked in the Valley of the Kings even went on strike when they weren't supplied.

FRANKINCENSE: PERFUME OF THE GODS

By Greek and Roman times perfume and incense spices were viewed as essential for every religious ritual or social occasion. They were given as offerings and burnt on the altars of the gods. Frankincense was one of the most highly valued of all the perfume spices. It was used in worship, and at weddings. The tree from which frankincense was obtained – *Boswellia sacra* – grew only in what is now Oman.

Trade there was so fraught with danger and cost that stories evolved about flying snakes which infested the trees from which the spice was collected.

SCENTS OF THE ANCIENT WORLD

Many scents known and valued in the ancient world are still used. Musk, taken from the sexual glands of one particular species of deer, was known by 400 AD.

Camphor was also sought after in the ancient world; for example, used to preserve bodies in Sumatra. Christ is said to have been anointed with camphor at the wedding in Canaan, an expense that other guests in the story complain about. Today, camphor is still used in perfume and ointments.

SPICES AS APHRODISIACS

SPICE AND SEX

Spices, scent and sexuality were closely associated in the ancient world. Many spices, whatever other properties they had, were regarded as aphrodisiacs. It's a belief that lives on in the currency and lexicon of the English language, where spicy still implies something more than just flavour.

LOVE GAMES

In earliest literature and legends describing the love games and courtships of royalty, spices often play a part. According to ancient Chinese folklore the young eighth-century emperor, Jing Zong, fired paper darts scented with camphor and musk at his concubines. In the *Book of Proverbs* an adulteress spreads her bed with myrrh, aloeswood and cinnamon, saying to her lover, 'Come let us drink deep of love.'

APHRODISIACS

Surprisingly for the modern-day cook, one of the most aphrodisiac spices was thought in ancient times to be long pepper. Pliny records that the Emperor Augustus' daughter Julia took this pepper every day. Her immense sexual appetite was so notorious that her father had her banished.

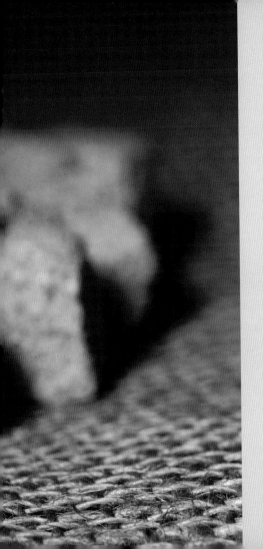

THE POTENCY OF SUGAR

Sugar was another spice believed to increase sexual power. Until the days of slavery and the sugar plantations it was a rare spice known to just a few. The only sweetener most people had access to was honey. In ancient Indian medical manuals sugar is said to have 'increased' the semen of those who chewed the fresh cane.

According to the ancients, one of the most potent and exotic of ancient spices was sandalwood. Used to enhance sexual attraction by the first millennium BC, in common with many spices it has never lost its sensual connotation.

A TASTE OF HISTORY
THE EARLY YEARS

Spices link us with history. Evidence of their use has been found in some of the earliest human settlements.
For example, in one cave in southern Greece, near Portokheli, archaeologists found a coriander seed – in a layer of debris reckoned to be 9,000 years old.

Ginger is also an ancient spice. Linguistic detective work, which can trace the movement of peoples through the survival of their languages, can pinpoint ginger's earliest cultivation to the peoples of southeastern China. Some 6,000 years ago these people transplanted ginger as they migrated across the Indian and Pacific oceans.

SPICES IN ANCIENT EGYPT

The ancient Egyptians are known to have been using spices found around the Mediterranean, such as cumin, coriander, poppy seed and aniseed, in 3500 BC. They were not only cooking with spices, but using them to embalm their dead. They also put spices into the tombs of the dead, along with the other equipment, food, clothes and servants that the dead were believed to need in the journey through the afterlife.

By 2000 BC spices had become valued commodities traded across the world, and Egypt was the centre of a lucrative market for incense and ritual

spices such as frankincense and myrrh. Egyptian ships sailed into the Persian Gulf to the mouth of the Euphrates to trade spices. At one temple outside what is now Luxor, a set of carved reliefs describes a journey by Queen Hatshepsut to the land of Punt, probably in what is now Somalia. Of the things the carvings boast of, spices are the most important.

THE SPICE ROUTES

On land, new trade routes opened up across Afghanistan and Persia, bringing in spices from the Malabar coast in southern India and Sri Lanka. Caravans carried spices across the Arabian desert to the ports of the Mediterranean. Pepper, ginger, cardamom and turmeric were brought to Egypt by Arab traders.

These routes were well established as early as 1000 BC, when the Old Testament story of Joseph was set down in writing. Joseph, hated by his brothers, is sold to Arab traders on their way to Egypt, their camels loaded with spices.

Arab peoples, at the crossroads between East and West, were well placed to gain early control of the spice trade. For over 5,000 years, as the trade grew through the Middle East into the Mediterranean, Arab caravans carried silk, rare goods and spices like frankincense, cinnamon and ginger. The caravans were often huge – sometimes consisting of thousands of camels.

New sea routes for the spice trade were beginning to open up by the

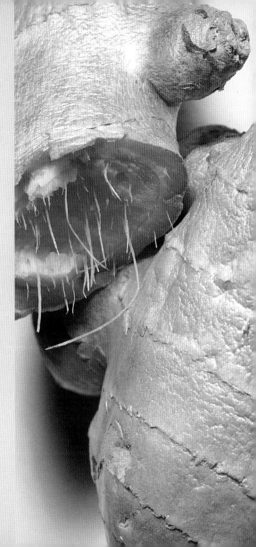

first century BC. The Greek sailor Hippalus is credited with discovering what Arab and Indian sailors may have already known – that ships could use the monsoon winds to cross the Indian Ocean, without the need to hug the coast. It meant a revolution in the trade between East and West. Arab merchants continued to be important, but now many different races – Jews, Indians, Persians, Chinese, Malay and Greeks – were recorded in the Indian ocean trade.

THE ROMAN EMPIRE

The Romans loved spices of every kind. They used the new sea routes and secured land routes to supply their insatiable desire for spices. Always attracted by the exotic and luxurious, they found many uses for spices: in cooking, in scenting rooms, in rituals and in celebration.

Throughout the day, rich Romans surrounded themselves with the scents and aromas of spices. Recipes show how seriously they took their gastronomy, demanding the most expensive luxuries in a single dish. It became a sign of wealth to consume spices in excessive quantities. The emperor Nero, after murdering his wife, burnt a year's supply of Rome's cinnamon as an offering at her funeral.

By the fifth century AD Rome's power was beginning to disintegrate. Rome was besieged by Alaric the Visigoth – who demanded not only gold but 3,000 pounds of pepper as ransom for the city.

A TASTE OF HISTORY
THE MIDDLE AGES

After Roman power disintegrated, Europe sank into the uncertainty of the dark ages. Much Greek and Roman knowledge of spices was lost but in the East the spice trade thrived. Arab merchants traded on routes that stretched from India and Sri Lanka to what is now Indonesia and China. The Malabar coast in southern India continued to grow in importance as a trading centre because it was close to the source of pepper, which would still account for some 70% of the world trade in spices in the 1500s.

THE ADVENTURES OF MARCO POLO

In Europe the scarcity of spices only increased their value. The new city states of Italy, such as Venice and Genoa, grew rich channelling spice from the Arab routes, but there was still no knowledge as to how a direct trade could be established.

In 1256 Marco Polo was born into a family of Venetian jewel merchants. Fascinated by the East, he travelled to China where he became the emissary for the Mongol emperor Kublai Khan. He began a series of journeys across the spice lands of China, Asia and India that lasted 24 years. When he returned to Venice he wrote his now famous *Adventures of Marco Polo*. It was a work that inspired generations of merchants and explorers that came after him.

AGE OF DISCOVERY

At the beginning of the 1500s, the extent of European ignorance and superstition of the wider world was immense. Many of the old merchants' tales of monsters and fierce races on the edge of the world, where the sources of spice were to be found, were still believed. It was not understood, for example, that plants could sometimes grow beyond their native habitats – a fact of great significance when it came to spices. Or that ships could use monsoon and trade winds to cross oceans.

European seafarers, increasingly obsessed with the fabulous wealth of the spice trade, were desperate to find a sea route to India and the East. However, Europeans were disadvantaged by their poor

understanding of sailing and climate. While European sailors survived on stinking rations, Malay and Chinese traders, whose junks and jongs were like floating cities, carried with them hundreds of men and their families, with room for fruit and vegetable gardens on board.

The discoveries of the 1500s changed everything. Twenty years after Vasco da Gama rounded Africa and found a sea route to India, Portugal had gained control of a large slice of the spice trade. Malacca, a fortress port guarding the vital spice routes between the South China Sea and the Indian Ocean, was taken in 1511.

After the capture of Malacca the Portuguese made their way to the Spice Islands. For the first time

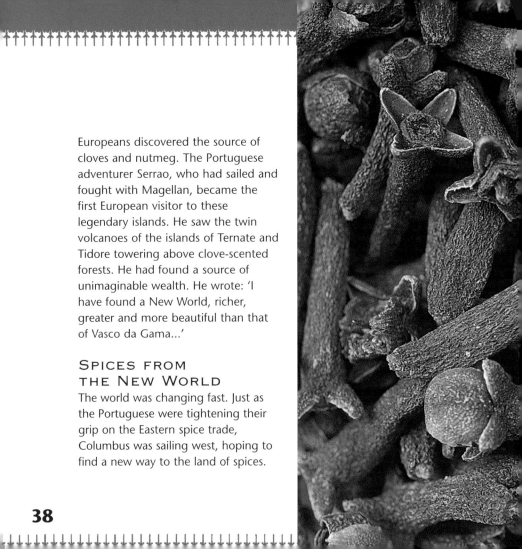

Europeans discovered the source of cloves and nutmeg. The Portuguese adventurer Serrao, who had sailed and fought with Magellan, became the first European visitor to these legendary islands. He saw the twin volcanoes of the islands of Ternate and Tidore towering above clove-scented forests. He had found a source of unimaginable wealth. He wrote: 'I have found a New World, richer, greater and more beautiful than that of Vasco da Gama...'

SPICES FROM THE NEW WORLD

The world was changing fast. Just as the Portuguese were tightening their grip on the Eastern spice trade, Columbus was sailing west, hoping to find a new way to the land of spices.

He didn't discover a new spice route, but a new world. He returned with chilli, which was to transform eating habits worldwide.

The journey of other spices was more limited, as various trading nations tried to establish monopolies. The Portuguese established a tight monopoly on nutmegs and cloves. With such fabulous wealth at stake, the Portuguese had stiff competition and were soon displaced by the Dutch who, in turn, vied for possession and control of the Spice Islands with the British. It was here, in 1602, that the British took control of their first colonial possession, a small island called Run. When the Dutch seized it back in 1621 they gave in return, as a treaty concession, the Dutch fort at New Amsterdam – now New York.

A TASTE OF HISTORY
THE MODERN AGE

The Dutch were ruthless in their attempts to control the spice trade. After regaining control of Run from the British they slaughtered every adult male on the island, and uprooted every nutmeg tree. Nearby, clove trees from Ternate and Tidore were transplanted to more easily defended islands, and the native clove industry was wiped out. Back in Amsterdam stocks of spices held in warehouses were burnt in order to protect prices.

VICIOUS RIVALRY

However, Dutch dominance of the spice trade was always precarious. There was simply too much money to be made and so a vicious and bloody rivalry developed between the British and the Dutch. Both kingdoms commissioned companies – the British and Dutch East India Companies – whose sole aim was to exploit the spice trade. There were countless skirmishes between ships trading around the Spice Islands – which the Dutch claimed as their own. Prisoners, who were often held as bargaining chips, were treated with none of the usual etiquette. The Dutch held one British crew, captured off the island of Run, in cells with iron-grilled roofs which were used as toilets by their jailers. The bloody rivalry between the Dutch and British was to continue for 200 years, with the British gaining control of India and Sri Lanka and the Dutch Java and Sumatra.

PETER PIPER PICKED

It was not until the late eighteenth century that the Dutch monopoly of the spice trade was broken, partly through the extraordinary perseverance of one Frenchman. Pierre Poivre had lost an arm in a naval engagement with the British, surviving gangrene and amputation on a burning ship, and been imprisoned for a year in China before getting an appointment as a French colonial administrator.

Pierre Poivre – whose name means pepper and who is probably the inspiration behind the tongue twister 'Peter Piper picked a peck of pickled peppers' – risked his life many times to secure seeds and seedlings from the Dutch nutmeg and clove islands.

Transplanting cloves or nutmegs was punished with death by the Dutch, and yet Poivre overcame mutinies, official obstruction and sabotage in his twenty-year quest. He eventually secured hundreds of nutmeg and clove seedlings which were planted in Mauritius, Madagascar, Zanzibar and the Caribbean.

AN ADVENTURER'S TRADE

The romance and profits of the spice trade attracted adventurers and visionaries. One of the first Americans to enter the spice trade successfully was Boston-born Eli Yale. He arrived in Madras in 1672 as a clerk with the British East India Company and went on to build a fortune in the spice trade – his wealth was used to found the world-famous Yale University.

SALEM CLIPPERS

The Americans entered the spice trade in force in the late 1800s. Clippers, fast sailing ships designed to carry cargo, began to make the 26,000-mile round trip to Sumatra and China. Sailing from the ports of Salem and Boston, they traded mostly in pepper. At the height of the trade, in the early nineteenth century, two or three ships a month put to sea to trade in spice. Their captains, men such as Jonathan Carnes, became famous, as their two- or three-year voyages into danger brought profits that made the ship owners millionaires.

THE SPICE TRADE TODAY

Today the US is the world's largest importer of spices – and not just black pepper. US Government statistics show that over 40 different spices and herbs are imported in vast and increasing quantities.

The role and importance of spices has changed throughout history. Today they are used – sometimes as essences – in low-calorie convenience foods, to add flavour and interest. They are also used in blends in all types of convenience food in order to give a brand distinctiveness and flavour. In the modern age they are used on a commercial and industrial scale that would amaze the traders and merchants of the ancient world.

STORAGE

Spices should be bought and used when their flavours are at their best. Many should be stored for as short a time as possible. If you need to store them one answer is to chop or purée the spices and then freeze them in sealed containers. They will keep for several months.

USE WHOLE SPICES

For most spices – from berries to bark and seeds – look to buy the whole seed, berry or pod. This is often the way to get the best-quality spices, ones that you know are unadulterated and unmixed. Also aim to grind, crush or grate the spice only when it's required. This process releases the important flavours of the spice – and afterwards it is only a matter of time before flavour and power are lost.

KEEP AIRTIGHT

Keep spices whole in airtight containers, away from heat and sunlight. If you're using ready-ground spices keep them this way for around six months. Test freshness by smelling and looking at the spices – if they're at all musty, have lost their colour, or don't smell much, they're past their best.

LONG KEEPERS

Some spices can keep their taste and usefulness for a considerable time. Mustard powder, for instance, needs water to activate the particular enzyme which contributes to its flavour. As a powder it will keep for over a year. Vanilla, cloves and tamarind will also keep for years rather than months.

COMMON NAME
ALLSPICE

GENUS SPECIES
Pimenta dioica

FAMILY
Myrtaceae

ORIGIN
Jamaica, Central and
South America

DESCRIPTION

Allspice, sometimes called Jamaican pepper, is the berry of an evergreen tropical tree. When dried, the berries resemble large, brown peppercorns. Allspice has the flavour of cloves, cinnamon and nutmeg – the combination explains its name. It is used in puddings and cakes, and in French cuisine in terrines and pâtés. In the Middle East it is used mainly in savoury food, with rice or minced meat. In Scandinavia it is used in pickling fish such as herrings.

The allspice tree can grow to 12 m (40 ft), and has white flowers. The berries are purple when ripe, but are picked when green. Every part of the tree has a heavy, spicy scent.

Allspice has been traded since the time of Columbus, who, when he was hoping to find pepper, was introduced to the spice in what is now Jamaica. It was used by Caribbean peoples to flavour food, and by the Mayan Indians in embalming.

PURCHASE AND USE

It is possible to buy ground allspice, but the spice keeps its flavour better whole, and is best bought as whole berries and ground when needed.

49

ANISEED

 GENUS SPECIES
Pimpinella anisum

 FAMILY
Apiaceae

 ORIGIN
Eastern
Mediterranean

DESCRIPTION

Aniseed, sometimes called anise or sweet cumin, is a short, annual plant, from the same family as parsley. Its tiny, oval seeds have a sweet, liquorice flavour. Aniseed is widely used in central European cooking, particularly as a flavouring for breads, while in India it is widely used with fish. Aniseed is also familiar as a flavouring for sweets, and various aniseed-flavoured drinks, from the French pastis to Turkish raki and Greek ouzo.

Aniseed spread from its native eastern Mediterranean to the rest of southern and central Europe during the Middle Ages. It was even grown in Britain, though it prefers warm climates. Star anise is a very different plant from true aniseed, though it tastes almost identical. Star anise is an evergreen tropical tree. Its fruit opens into an eight-pointed star, and both fruit husk and the seeds inside are ground and used as spice. Star anise is one of the most important spices in Chinese cuisine – and is used with pork and duck in particular.

PURCHASE AND USE

It's possible to buy aniseed whole. It can be gently heated or dry-fried to bring out its flavour before being added to food. An easier and more convenient way to add it is as a concentrate in a liquid form, such as pastis or ouzo.

COMMON NAME
ASAFOETIDA

DESCRIPTION
Asafoetida is a large annual plant that can grow to over 1.8 m (6 ft), and looks like cow parsley or giant fennel. The spice itself comes from the dried sap of the swollen root. Asafoetida is unusual because its aroma is highly unpleasant – it has been variously known since Greek and Roman times as stink finger and devil's dung.

When cooked, its smell disappears and it develops a mild onion flavour. It is commonly used in Indian vegetable cooking and with pulses and pickles, partly because of its reputation as a cure for flatulence.

GENUS SPECIES
Ferula asafoetida

FAMILY
Umbelliferae

ORIGIN
Central Asia

Asafoetida was brought to Europe from what is now Afghanistan and Iran by the armies of Alexander the Great. It is thought that its flavour resembles silphium, one of the Roman Empire's most prized, and rarest, spices. When the true silphium, once native to the Mediterranean area, became extinct, asafoetida was used as an alternative. Throughout Roman times it was used extensively as a flavouring and as a remedy.

PURCHASE AND USE

Asafoetida is most often sold as a powder, and sometimes as a waxy resin. It's best used in small quantities with vegetable dishes where it can be a rewarding and pleasant alternative to onion or garlic.

53

COMMON NAME
BLACK PEPPER

GENUS SPECIES
Piper nigrum

FAMILY
Piperaceae

ORIGIN
Southern India

DESCRIPTION

Pepper is the small, round berry of a climbing vine. The green and unripe berries are picked and dried in the sun, where they shrivel and harden into the familiar black peppercorns.

From ancient times pepper was one of the most precious of spices. The Romans valued it more highly than gold. When Rome was sacked by the Visigoths, they demanded a tribute that included not just gold and silver, but also pepper.

The pepper first traded was long pepper, which is slightly hotter than the pepper of today, and much harder to grow. Long pepper, which can only

be found in India and Indonesia today, was probably southern India's most valuable export for some 2,000 years.

PURCHASE AND USE
Once it's ground, pepper quickly loses part of its flavour. It is best bought whole, and ground when required.

There are several kinds of pepper available. White pepper is from the same plant as black pepper, but the berries are allowed to ripen and turn red. The husks are then removed to leave clean, white berries. White pepper has a very similar taste to black pepper. Green peppercorns are not dried but preserved or frozen.

COMMON NAME
CARAWAY

 GENUS SPECIES
Carum carvi

 FAMILY
Umbelliferae

 ORIGIN
Europe and Central Asia

DESCRIPTION
Caraway is biennial, flowering every two years. Its black, slightly curved seeds are widely used in German, Austrian and Scandinavian cooking.

Caraway's feathery leaves can be chopped and eaten. They are added to food in the same way as parsley. The roots can also be eaten – they are cooked in the same way as parsnips.

Caraway is from the same family as dill and fennel, and it has the same kind of round, hollow stems and feathery leaves. It has been found by archaeologists in sites dating back

5,000 years. Caraway was used by the ancient Egyptians in the tombs of the dead to ward off evil spirits. It was also used in bread by the Romans, and since medieval times it has been used to flavour cheese.

PURCHASE AND USE

Caraway can be bought as seed. It is sometimes confused with cumin, as the seeds look similar, and the two spices share the same name in some languages. In German, for instance, kümmel refers to both caraway and cumin. Even so, the two spices have very different flavours.

57

CARDAMOM

DESCRIPTION

Cardamom is a small, green seed pod. It grows from a perennial plant from the same family as ginger. Cardamom is an important ingredient in curry powders, and in garam masala. It is also used in many Indian sweetmeats and puddings. In Scandinavia it is used to flavour liqueurs and a variety of foods from pickled herrings to pastries. In the Middle East it is also used in food, and as a flavouring for coffee.

Cardamom was prized by the Greeks and Romans as a perfume. It subsequently gained a reputation in the Middle East as an aphrodisiac and stimulant.

GENUS SPECIES
Elettaria
cardamomum

FAMILY
Zingiberaceae

ORIGIN
Southern India and
Sri Lanka

PURCHASE AND USE

Cardamom pods are best bought whole. The pods should be unsplit, and the small, black seeds inside should be slightly sticky with a strong aromatic smell. Once the pods are opened and the seeds exposed, cardamom will quickly lose its flavour.

There are three kinds of cardamom available. Green cardamom has the finest flavour while white cardamom are the same pods, but bleached. Black cardamom pods are larger, have a stronger, rougher flavour and are often used in highly spiced Indian cooking.

CHILLIES

Capsicum annuum

Solanaceae

Mexico

DESCRIPTION

Chillies are the fiery fruit of the chilli plant. There are more than 100 varieties, from the small and dangerously hot habanero to the more mild, sweet chillies, such as the choricero or Spanish chilli.

Probably the world's most popular spice, chillies are an essential part of the culinary tradition of the Americas, the Caribbean, India and Asia. The heat comes from capsaicin. Its effects and strength vary according to the variety, and there is even a scale used to categorise the heat of chillies.

Chillies are a native plant of Mexico. They have probably been used from

the wild for more than 7,000 years
and cultivated for around 6,000 years.

PURCHASE AND USE

Using fresh chillies, which can be
green, red, orange or yellow, is
sometimes a matter of guesswork,
since it is hard to tell from looking at a
chilli how hot it is. As a general rule,
the smaller the chilli the hotter it is.
Never touch your lips or eyes after you
have been handling fresh chillies.

Chillies are also often sold dried, but
the easiest way to use them is as chilli
powder. While excellent for adding
hotness to food, powders don't give
the range or depth of flavours offered
by fresh chillies.

COMMON NAME

CINNAMON

DESCRIPTION

Cinnamon is the dried inner bark of an evergreen tree from the same family as laurel. It is used with meat and rice and vegetable dishes, especially in food from India, Turkey and Egypt.

In the US and Britain ground cinnamon is often used in sweet food, in cakes, pastries, biscuits, and particularly with fruit such as apples. Cinnamon is also often combined with chocolate and with spiced wines.

Cinnamon is cultivated as a bush. The slender outer branches are stripped of their outer bark, and cuts are made so that the inner bark lifts away. When the inner bark is dried, it becomes curled up quills or sticks.

GENUS SPECIES
Cinnamomum
zeylanicum

FAMILY
Lauraceae

ORIGIN
Sri Lanka

The use of cinnamon – or at least its close relative, cassia – is recorded in China from 2500 BC, and later in ancient Egypt, where it was used in embalming. Archaeologists have also found cinnamon on the Greek island of Samos, in finds dated to 700 BC. In *The Bible*, stories tell of it being valued more highly than gold.

PURCHASE AND USE
Cinnamon is best bought in small quantities and not stored for too long. It is possible to buy it ground, but the best-quality cinnamon is sold in stick, or quill, form.

COMMON NAME
CLOVES

GENUS SPECIES
Eugenia caryophyllis

FAMILY
Myrtaceae

ORIGIN
Moluccas

DESCRIPTION

Cloves are the dried flower buds of a tropical evergreen tree. The small, black buds have a powerful aromatic flavour. They are used in curry powders, in Chinese five spice, and often with fruit and meat. Eugenol, extracted from cloves, is used in toothpastes and mouthwashes. Much of the world's production of cloves is used in clove-flavoured cigarettes which are popular in Indonesia.

The clove tree can grow to some 9 m (30 ft). The fresh buds are pink, and turn red-brown as they are dried. Cloves look a little like nails – and are called the nail spice in both French and Chinese.

Cloves have been traded around the world for more than 3,500 years. They were one of the most valuable and widely known spices traded on the caravan routes from Asia. There have been finds dated to 1700 BC in the kitchens of ordinary households in Mesopotamia – now part of Iraq.

PURCHASE AND USE

Cloves are best bought whole. Their flavour is so strong that quality is less important than with many spices – though at their best cloves should be oily and plump rather than shrivelled.

65

CORIANDER

 GENUS SPECIES
Coriandrum sativum

 FAMILY
Apiaceae

 ORIGIN
Greece and the Eastern Mediterranean

DESCRIPTION

Coriander is a small, flat-leafed annual, from the same family as parsley. The leaves and round, yellow-brown seeds are used as a flavouring in a huge range of Indian and southeast Asian cooking. Coriander is a major ingredient in most curry powders, and in garam masala. In Thailand, cooks use coriander root, while the spice is popular in British and American pickles and in North African cuisine. It is also used in breads.

Coriander is mentioned in the *Book of Exodus*, and was one of the spices found in Tutankhamen's tomb. Archaeologists have also found coriander in ancient caves in southern Greece – finds dated to 9,000 years ago.

PURCHASE AND USE

Coriander is extremely versatile – its flavour works well on its own, and in combination with other spices. Any authentic Indian or southeast Asian dish uses coriander – often as ground seed, as well as in its green leaf form.

Both seeds and ground coriander have a pleasing mild taste, and are sold separately or combined with cumin in garam masala. To bring out the best flavour, coriander seeds should be heated gently in oil, or dry-fried in a pan, before they are added to food.

COMMON NAME
CUMIN

GENUS SPECIES
Cuminum cyminum

FAMILY
Apiaceae

ORIGIN
Eastern Mediterranean

68

DESCRIPTION

Cumin is a small, annual plant from the same family as parsley. It is the little, oblong, grey-green seeds of the plant that are used as a spice. Cumin's strong, slightly bitter, taste is an essential ingredient in Indian, Middle Eastern and north African cooking. It is also added to Mexican meat dishes such as chilli con carne, and to German foods like sauerkraut. It is sometimes used with cheese and in cheese making, as for example in Münster cheese.

Cumin originated around the Mediterranean, and spread eastwards, possibly following the conquests of Alexander the Great. It reached India more than 2,000 years ago. There is a surviving Roman recipe that includes it in a sauce for fish, and it was also ground into a paste and used as a spread on bread. According to Pliny, oil from the seed could be used by students to convince their teachers that they were working harder than they really were.

PURCHASE AND USE

Ground cumin is often combined with coriander and is essential in much Indian cooking. It is frequently combined in garam masala, which is used as a basis for many curry dishes. A black cumin, with smaller seeds, is grown in Iran.

COMMON NAME

CURRY LEAVES

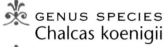
GENUS SPECIES
Chalcas koenigii

FAMILY
Rutaceae

ORIGIN
India

DESCRIPTION

Curry leaves come from a tropical tree of the same family as lemon – in fact lemon can be grafted onto the curry tree. The dark, waxy leaves have a strong, aromatic curry flavour.
Curry leaves should not be confused with curry powder, which is discussed on page 98.

The curry tree is grown widely across India. Its peculiar curry flavour is used in Madras-style curry powders and much Madras cooking. It lends an individual flavour unobtainable from spice mixtures or other spices.
Curry leaves are often fried in hot oil, or ghee with mustard seeds, and added to lentil dishes such as dhal.

70

PURCHASE AND USE

Curry leaves can be bought fresh.
Use them chopped, or add them
whole and take them out before
serving. Curry leaves can also be
bought and stored frozen, and
although you can sometimes find the
dried leaves they keep little of their
original strength unless they are
properly dried and vacuum-packed.

COMMON NAME
FENUGREEK

GENUS SPECIES
Trigonella
foenum-graecum

FAMILY
Fabaceae

ORIGIN
India and Southern
Europe

DESCRIPTION

Fenugreek is a green, round-leaved annual. The plant, which grows to around 50 cm (19 in.), has small, white flowers and a soft, mild flavour of curry. Both the green leaves and the small yellow seeds, which grow in pods, are used as a flavouring and as a vegetable. Commercially, fenugreek seeds are used in chutneys and in some curry powders.

Fenugreek grows wild across north Africa. In some countries it is grown as a fodder crop. It is a useful plant because it restores nitrogen to the soil.

Fenugreek is rich in vitamins and minerals. As a green leaf, it is an

important ingredient in Indian lentil and vegetable dishes where the leaves, used fresh and dried, are known as 'methi'.

PURCHASE AND USE

Fenugreek seeds are very hard, and must be ground before they are eaten. When raw, they have very little flavour, and need to be roasted or fried – but gently, since if they are overcooked they turn red and bitter.

Fresh leaf fenugreek is extremely nutritious, but tends to be bitter eaten on its own. Fenugreek seeds can be sprouted, are rich in vitamins and can be eaten raw as a salad in the same way as mustard or cress.

COMMON NAME
GARLIC

 GENUS SPECIES
Allium sativum

 FAMILY
Alliaceae

 ORIGIN
Probably Central Asia

74

DESCRIPTION

Garlic is a perennial bulb. There are several varieties, from the small, pinkish-skinned garlic grown in France, to the giant, white variety grown in California. The bulbs break into cloves, which have a fine pink-to-white papery skin. Garlic is an essential flavour in some of the world's best food, from China and India to the Mediterranean.

Garlic was found in the tomb of Tutankhamen and was given to the workers building the Pyramids. In Chinese tradition garlic was believed to ward off evil. Roman soldiers chewed garlic as a stimulant before going into battle.

Garlic contains natural antiseptic and antibiotic properties and is reputed to help lower blood pressure and blood cholesterol.

PURCHASE AND USE

Garlic is harvested in late summer – and this is often when it is at its best. Fresh garlic should be hard and firm, and the cloves creamy-white and juicy. Brownish spots or a faded, dry appearance are a sign that the garlic is past its best. If you have to use cloves like this, cut off any brown spots.

Garlic can be chopped, grated or crushed. If only a hint of garlic is needed it can be rubbed over the food before it is cooked.

COMMON NAME

GINGER

GENUS SPECIES
Zingiber officinale

FAMILY
Zingiberaceae

ORIGIN
Southern China

DESCRIPTION

Ginger is the bulbous, fleshy root of the ginger plant. The roots can be used fresh, dried or pickled. In Europe and America, ginger in its dried powder form is traditionally used in sweet foods and drinks, while in Indian and east Asian food, fresh ginger is used whole, grated, chopped, crushed, shredded or in marinades.

The ginger plant grows to about 1 m (3 ft), has long leaves, and attractive, white or yellow flowers. The roots have a thin, silvery skin, and a characteristically knotty appearance.

Ginger originates from southern China. Mentioned in the writings of

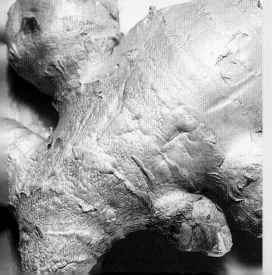

Confucius (c. 500 BC), ginger is probably one of the oldest known spices – linguistic detective work traces its earliest journeys to the ancient peoples of southeast China.

PURCHASE AND USE

Fresh ginger root should be plump, with smooth, thin, silvery skin, and not too fibrous. Wrinkled or soft roots are not fresh. Young, tender roots are the best of all.

Ginger root can also be bought pickled and preserved, or as syrupy sweet stem ginger. Ground, powdered ginger is ideal for baking, but as with many spices, the best way is to buy dried roots and grind them yourself.

77

COMMON NAME
LEMON GRASS

 GENUS SPECIES
Cymbopogon citratus

 FAMILY
Gramineae

 ORIGIN
Southeast Asia

DESCRIPTION

Lemon grass is a perennial, grassy plant, with long, sharp leaves and a swollen stem. It contains citral, one of the essential oils used to synthesise the flavour of lemon, but no citric acid. This gives lemon grass the fragrant quality of lemon without its sharpness.

Lemon grass is used as a flavouring in food across southeast Asia. It is most often combined with ginger, garlic and chillies, and with coconut milk. Its essential oil is used in perfumes and soaps.

78

Purchase and Use

Lemon grass stems are hard and need crushing before cooking. In most recipes they are taken out before the food is eaten. In dishes where the lemon grass is eaten, use only the tender, lower part of the stem, and slice it finely or grate it.

Fresh lemon grass will keep in a cool place for up to three weeks – or you can slice and freeze the lower part of the stems. If you can't find fresh lemon grass its dried, powder form is called sereh.

COMMON NAME

MUSTARD

 GENUS SPECIES
Brassica nigra,
Brassica juncea
Brassica alba

 FAMILY
Brassicaceae

 ORIGIN
Europe and Asia

DESCRIPTION

Mustard is made from the seeds of three plants of the cabbage family. It is widely used as a condiment, but also in curries, sauces and as oil in cooking across the world. Sprouted seeds can also be eaten as a salad.

Mustard was familiar in Greece at least 4,000 years ago – Pythagoras recommended it for the treatment of scorpion stings. It was probably the hottest flavour available in Europe until the beginning of the black pepper trade in around 400 BC. It has been enjoyed as a smooth paste or sauce for at least 2,000 years.

80

PURCHASE AND USE

The three basic kinds of mustard seed are white, brown and black. Each kind of mustard has a distinct flavour and characteristic, and is mixed and prepared differently.

American mustard is made with white mustard seeds and has the mildest taste. Sugar and other spices such as turmeric are added. English mustard, which is made with white mustard seeds and brown mustard for hotness and bite, is the hottest. Bordeaux mustard, often called French mustard, is one of many French varieties. It is a blend of black and brown seeds and husks and has a mild, sweet taste.

81

COMMON NAME

NUTMEG AND MACE

GENUS SPECIES
Myristica fragrans

FAMILY
Myristicaceae

ORIGIN
Moluccas

DESCRIPTION

Nutmeg is a large, hard, brown seed. It grows on an evergreen tropical tree inside a small soft fruit, a little like an apricot. Inside the fruit each nutmeg is wrapped in a brilliant red net, or aril, of mace, that spreads out, vein-like, around the nut.

Mace and nutmeg are dried and used separately. Both have a similar flavour, but mace is a little less sweet and traditionally used in savoury foods. Nutmeg and mace can be added to a huge variety of foods: in everything from sauces to sausages, with spinach, cheese and in biscuits and cakes.

In Elizabethan England – and still today in Malaysia and Indonesia – the fleshy fruit body of the nutmeg is eaten as candied fruit.

Nutmeg was a valued and costly perfume spice used in the Parthian court of the kings of Persia. It has been known and valued in Europe since Roman times. However, it was the French who transplanted nutmeg from the Moluccas, breaking a monopoly and changing the spice from a luxury into one of the most widely used spices in Europe.

PURCHASE AND USE

Nutmegs are best bought whole, and grated when required. They are also a mild narcotic – and have a reputation as an aphrodisiac.

COMMON NAME

PAPRIKA

GENUS SPECIES
Capsicum annuum

FAMILY
Solanaceae

ORIGIN
South America

DESCRIPTION

Paprika is a bright red powder made from dried sweet peppers. It is an essential ingredient in Hungarian meat and chicken dishes, such as goulash. In Spain, where it is known as pimenton, paprika is widely used in foods such as sobrasada sausage. The Spanish also use dried whole peppers in a rich variety of sauces.

Paprika was first made in Hungary, from sweet capsicum peppers brought by the Turks. Although the long, pointed red peppers are related to chilli peppers, paprika has little of the heat of chilli, and the core and seeds are removed when the peppers are dried, which further reduces the heat.

Paprika has a mild, sweet taste. Hungarian and Spanish paprika often vary as they are made from different varieties of sweet capsicum pepper.

PURCHASE AND USE
Buy paprika when you want to use it, since it will go stale if kept for too long. Good, fresh paprika is a brilliant red – if the powder has a brownish colour it may well be stale. Unlike some spices, paprika is best used liberally; sprinkling it on food is only useful as decoration. It is rich in vitamin C.

85

POPPY SEEDS

GENUS SPECIES
Papaver somniferum

FAMILY
Papaveraceae

ORIGIN
Middle East

DESCRIPTION

The tiny, black seeds used in cooking are the edible seeds of the opium poppy. The opium poppy grows to around 1 m (3 ft), with large, pretty flowers that vary in colour from lilac to white. The ripe seeds have been used in cooking and baking across the Middle East and Europe since ancient Greek times. A poppy seed bread is mentioned in a Greek text 2,600 years old.

Poppy seeds have a pleasant, nutty taste when baked or heated. Different culinary traditions use them sprinkled on baked breads and cakes. In India, white poppy seeds (called khus-khus) – from a different kind of poppy, but

with a very similar flavour – are used ground as a thickener for curries. In Russian tradition, ground black seeds are mixed with honey and used as a cake filling. A clear, edible oil is also extracted from poppy seeds – as well as a lower-quality reddish oil used in artists' paints.

PURCHASE AND USE

Poppy seeds don't keep indefinitely so are best bought and used when required. Apart from baking and bread, poppy seeds can be added as flavour and texture to dressings and salads. They work well when added to mashed vegetables. Poppy seeds can also be sprouted and used as a salad.

SAFFRON

DESCRIPTION

Saffron is the dried stigmas from the flower of the saffron crocus. A tiny pinch of these bright red-orange strands gives food colour and flavour. Saffron combines well with the flavours of fish and garlic, and is used in Mediterranean dishes such as paella. It is also used in Indian sweetmeats and special rice dishes, and in France as an ingredient in the liqueur Chartreuse.

The saffron crocus is autumn-flowering. Each crocus flower has three stigmas, and each of these must be picked by hand. Just one pound of saffron can contain up to 250,000 stigmas.

 GENUS SPECIES
Crocus sativus

 FAMILY
Iridaceae

 ORIGIN
Greece and Asia Minor

Saffron was prized by the ancient Greeks, the Persians and the Romans. Arab traders introduced the saffron crocus to Spain – where much of the world's best saffron still comes from.

PURCHASE AND USE

Saffron is sometimes adulterated with turmeric, marigold or safflower – all of which have colour but not the pungent taste of saffron. It is best to buy the bright red-orange strands, rather than the powder. They will be slightly ragged, without light patches, and each stigma will expand immediately when put onto the surface of hot water. Use saffron sparingly – most dishes will never need more than a quarter or half a teaspoon.

89

SESAME

 GENUS SPECIES
Sesamum indicum

 FAMILY
Pedaliaceae

 ORIGIN
India

DESCRIPTION

Sesame is a tropical annual that can grow to 1.8 m (6 ft). When roasted, its tiny, flat seeds have a beautiful nutty taste. They are used in Japanese and Asian cooking – for example, scattered on crackers. In Middle Eastern tradition they are a major ingredient in hummus, and are used to make a sweet sugar cake called halva. Sesame is also used as cooking oil and in margarine.

Sesame plants have finger-shaped, pink or white flowers – depending on the variety – and hairy leaves. The seeds vary from brown to red, yellow and black. Sesame probably originated in India, but it has been known about, and used, worldwide for thousands of years. It features in the story of Ali Baba, as the magic words 'open sesame'. The ancient Greeks, Egyptians and Persians used sesame. Some 5,000 years ago the Chinese were burning sesame oil to make soot for ink.

Today, sesame oil is used in ointments, soaps and cosmetics. It is a favourite cooking oil in many hot countries because it doesn't turn rancid in heat.

PURCHASE AND USE

Sesame oil is readily available and is an essential flavouring in Chinese and Far Eastern cooking. Sesame seeds can also be bought whole and used in cooking.

91

COMMON NAME
TAMARIND

 GENUS SPECIES
Tamarindus indica

 FAMILY
Fabaceae

 ORIGIN
East Africa or India

DESCRIPTION
Tamarind, sometimes called Indian date, is prepared from the ripe, brown seed pod of a large, evergreen tropical tree. Its sour-sweet flavour is widely used in Indian and southeast Asian cooking, especially in lentil dishes and chutneys. It is also used commercially as a basis for fruit drinks – and in Worcestershire sauce.

Tamarind seed pods are about the same size and appearance as brown, broad bean pods. The sticky red-brown, stringy pulp inside the seed pod contains the sugar and tartaric acid which gives tamarind its sourness.

Tamarind has been cultivated in India for centuries, and was probably also native in east Africa. It was known in Europe by medieval times, and the Spanish brought it to the Caribbean in the sixteenth century. It is still used in India for its medicinal properties, particularly for stomach and bowel complaints.

PURCHASE AND USE

The easiest way to buy and use tamarind is as a concentrated paste or purée. Sometimes tamarind is sold fresh or as a compressed, partly dried block. Prepare this kind of tamarind by soaking the sticky, brown pulp in boiling water, and pushing the softened pulp, minus the seeds, through a sieve.

COMMON NAME
TURMERIC

GENUS SPECIES
Curcuma longa

FAMILY
Zingiberaceae

ORIGIN
Southeast Asia

DESCRIPTION

Turmeric is most often available as a ground, bright yellow powder, and is an ingredient in curry powders, mustards and relishes such as piccalilli.

The spice is the root of a tropical perennial plant and has large lily-like leaves and yellow flowers. The roots are bright orange, turning to yellow as they are dried.

In southern India, turmeric has been used in ritual and in food for more than 2,000 years. It is still important in Hindu wedding ceremonies, where a thread dipped in turmeric paste is tied around the neck of the bride.

Turmeric has antiseptic properties, and in Malaysia a paste made of turmeric is traditionally spread on the umbilical cord of a newborn child. In traditional Chinese medicine, it is used for controlling the clotting of blood. Turmeric is also used as a dye, for example, by the food industry for things such as butter.

PURCHASE AND USE
Turmeric has a mild, earthy taste. It can add colour and flavour to curries, dhal and Indian fish dishes such as kedgeree. In north African cooking it is added to lamb and vegetables. Dried turmeric root is difficult to grind, so it's best to buy it as a powder.

COMMON NAME
VANILLA

 GENUS SPECIES
Vanilla fragrans

 FAMILY
Orchidaceae

 ORIGIN
Central America

DESCRIPTION
Vanilla is the seed pod of a climbing tropical orchid. It is used to flavour cakes, puddings, liqueurs and chocolate.

Vanilla – often mixed with chocolate – was first used by the Aztecs in what is now Mexico. The Spanish brought dried vanilla pods to Europe, but for centuries it proved impossible to grow the pods anywhere outside its native Mexico.

The flowers of the vanilla orchid last for just one day, and can be pollinated by only one species of bee, and one species of hummingbird, both of which survive only in Mexico.

It wasn't until the 1840s that a way was perfected to pollinate the vanilla flower artificially, and vanilla was successfully grown outside Mexico.

The long, yellow pods are picked unripe, and have no flavour until sweated or cured in airtight boxes, and then dried. The difficulty in growing vanilla is one reason why it is so expensive.

PURCHASE AND USE

The best vanilla pods are dark brown, tough but still flexible. The pods can keep their intense, yet subtle, flavour for several years, and can be used many times, as long as they are washed and dried each time.

97

SPICE MIXTURES

Some spices are often sold as mixtures. They can be a convenient and easy way to create authentic-tasting dishes. The three most widely used are curry powder, garam masala and Chinese five spice.

CURRY POWDER

Curry powder is a mixture of spices which often – but not always – includes coriander, cloves, cumin, curry leaves, fenugreek, ginger, turmeric, mustard seeds, black pepper and chillies.

Curry powder doesn't reflect the subtlety or variety of actual Indian food, but it is convenient. What's more, the quality and variety of curry powders have improved as interest in food and cooking has grown. In Indian, and in Oriental cooking, curry powders are never or rarely used, but spices are combined according to the region, and the dish being prepared. For example, blends of spices used in southern India – Goa or Madras – are the hottest. North Indian cooking tends to concentrate on more aromatic flavours.

A classic southern Indian style mixture is sambaar, which is often used for lentil dishes. Bengali curry powder, or panch phoron, is equal quantities of unroasted cumin, fennel, mustard, fenugreek and nigella seeds. It can be fried in ghee (clarified butter) and added to lentil or vegetable dishes just before serving.

GARAM MASALA

Garam masala is the basis of many Indian dishes – and is most typical of north Indian cooking. Its name literally means warm spices. Garam masala varies, but will usually include coriander seed, cumin, cardamom, ground chilli and black pepper. Cinnamon, nutmeg and cloves are also often included.

Garam masala is often used in Indian home cooking – either home prepared in quantity and stored, or bought ready-mixed. The spices, in many cases, need to be gently roasted separately, so it makes sense to prepare more than is needed for one meal.

Garam masala is generally used as a
convenient basic flavouring for a dish.
Other spices will be added to finish
the flavour.

CHINESE FIVE SPICE

Chinese five spice is a familiar flavour
from Chinese cooking. As its name
suggests, five spice is an equal mixture
of five spices – star anise, cassia or
cinnamon, cloves, fennel seed and
Szechwan or anise pepper.

Chinese five spice – sometimes
just called five spice – is always a good
flavour for pork. It can also be used
with chicken, and in combination
with soy sauce.

101

GROWING SPICES

If you are only used to dried and packaged spices then growing them could be a revolutionary experience. There are many spices, that despite their exotic flavours and mysterious reputations, are easy to grow at home. Most only need a small patch of garden to flourish, or can usefully thrive in pots. Some can be eaten and used for cooking – others more used to tropical climates will survive inside as ornamental houseplants.

GARLIC

A small patch of soil in a sunny, well-drained spot is all you need. Garlic's flavour suffers in cold, damp climates – so beware in a bad summer.

- Prepare the ground, breaking the soil to a fine tilth.

- Break a bulb of garlic into separate cloves, and plant in rows 5 cm (2 in.) deep and 15 cm (6 in.) apart. In warm climates you can plant garlic in autumn, but in cold, frost-prone climates plant out in early spring.

- Garlic grows spikes of round, fleshy leaves. Keep them weeded and watered. In late summer, when the leaf spikes begin to turn brown and fold over, pull out the bulbs and leave them to dry, either out on the soil, or inside on some newspaper.

- Store garlic in a cool place – ideally hanging as plaits or in bunches.

CHILLIES

Chillies can grow outside in temperate climates, but you will need some luck and a sunny, sheltered spot. They are best grown under glass. Plants grow to around 1 m (3 ft).

- If it's hard to find chilli seed, save and dry seed from a fresh, store-bought chilli.

- Start the seeds in compost-filled pots – the seeds need only a light covering of compost. Germination will take 2–3 weeks.

- Chillies need well-drained, fertile soil or compost. Inside, start them in 22 cm (9 in.) pots, and repot as necessary.

- Raise seedlings at 18–24°C (65–75°F).

- Plant seedlings out in June in temperate climates – or in April–May under glass.

- Water regularly, but don't allow soil to become waterlogged.

- Stake and support plants as they grow, using manure to keep them fed.

- Expect the fruit to ripen from August. They can be picked green or red. How hot your home-grown chillies are will often depend on the weather – hot weather will mean hotter chillies.

GINGER

Ginger has long, attractive leaves, a little like those of the lily family, and beautiful white flowers. It's unlikely to produce roots good enough for cooking, but it makes an unusual houseplant all the same.

- The secret to propagating ginger easily is to find fresh and young ginger root. Look in an Oriental or Asian food store that sells spices in quantity. You're more likely to find fresh, good-quality ginger here than in supermarkets where it is usually wrapped in plastic and that much older. The root should be plump and fresh. Occasionally, it is even possible to find a root with ready-to-grow, firm, green shoots.

- Push the ginger root about 5 cm (2 in.) down into rich, moist compost. Use a medium-sized pot, that will drain well.

- Ginger needs a sunny, warm spot in the house. Keep the soil moist but not wet.

LEMON GRASS

Lemon grass has interesting grassy foliage.

- To propagate lemon grass first seek out the freshest stems from an Oriental grocer – these will occasionally have little buds on them.

- Start the stems off by standing them in a jar of water on a windowsill.

106

- When the buds begin to sprout, move the stems to moist compost.

- Keep the plants in a sunny, warm spot.

POPPY SEEDS

Poppies grow easily and make beautiful garden flowers. They also produce a plentiful supply of seeds for cooking, or sprouting, in the same way as mustard and fenugreek seeds.

- Buy seed of the giant poppy variety (its botanical name is *papaver somniferum*).

- Prepare soil in a sunny spot, working it to a fine tilth. It should be good, rich soil, dampened before planting.

107

- Either sow the poppies in shallow drills about 30 cm (12 in.) apart, or scatter the seed over the planting area.

- Cut the seed heads after the petals have fallen. Leave the seed heads to dry.

- Break the heads open to extract the seed – a quick way is to put the dried heads in a plastic bag, hold the top closed and shake the bag. You should be rewarded with a harvest of fine blue-grey seeds ideal for cooking or sprouting.

CORIANDER

Coriander is an attractive plant with small, feathery leaves and small, white flowers. It grows easily, both for seed and for its fresh leaf which is a distinctive and versatile cooking spice in its own right. The seed can be dried and ground for spice.

- Sow seeds in early spring in rows, in rich soil in full sun.

- Thin out the tiny plants after a few weeks.

- Cut the leaf as necessary.

- Coriander will quickly go to seed so plant staggered rows for a longer cropping season.

- For seed, let the plants stand though the summer. The small, round seeds turn light brown when ripe. Cut the plants, hang to dry for a few days, and then shake inside a plastic bag to free the seeds.

- Store in an airtight container and grind when required.

SPROUTED SEEDS

Many seed spices that are usually roasted and ground can also be sprouted. Used this way they make delicious and easy-to-grow, year-round salad. Sprouting only takes a few days, so it is a satisfying way to experiment with spices. Sprouted seeds are very rich in vitamins and minerals. They can be eaten raw as salad, or cooked – especially stir-fried.

- Seed for sprouting obviously needs to be viable, so check it is unroasted when you buy it.

- Seeds such as fenugreek and mustard make ideal sprouted seeds. They should be easy to find in shops selling a good range of spices.

- Wash the seeds in cold water, then put them in slightly warm water and soak them overnight. A few tablespoons of seed will make a generous salad. When sprouted they will increase around five times in volume.

- Drain the seed.

- For mustard seed, place the seeds on a flat tray on a few layers of paper towel. Put the tray in a warm place in the dark until the seeds germinate – the temperature

should be around 13–24°C (55–75°F). Then move into the light, but out of the Sun. Keep the tray damp but not wet. Harvest after 10–15 days, when the seedlings are around 5 cm (2 in.) high. The sprouts have a peppery flavour.

- Sprout fenugreek seeds in a jar, its top covered with a piece of muslin held in place with an elastic band. Keep in the dark till the seeds germinate. Rinse the seeds every day by part-filling the jar, and gently pouring the water off again through the muslin. When the seeds germinate bring into the light, and harvest after two days. The sprouts have a spicy flavour.

CHILLI SALSA

INGREDIENTS

6 ripe tomatoes
1 red onion
2 white onions
1 chilli (deseeded and finely
    chopped)
2 tbsp chopped coriander
1 green pepper, seeded and
    chopped
$1/2$ tsp chopped oregano
juice of 2 lemons
3 tbsp oil
$1/2$ tsp ground pepper
salt

Chilli sauce is a quick, fiery
accompaniment that's popular
throughout Latin America, and in
varied forms across Asia. This salsa can
be used as a dip or relish.

METHOD

1. Finely chop the tomatoes, onions
   and chilli.
2. Combine with the rest of
   the ingredients.

TIP

USE THIS CAJUN CHILLI MIX WITH
FISH STEAKS, CHICKEN OR MEAT.
THE PREPARED
SPICE INGREDIENTS CAN
BE KEPT FRESH IN AN AIRTIGHT
CONTAINER – ADD THE
GARLIC AND ONION WHEN YOU
USE THE MIX.

CAJUN CHILLI CHIPS

FOR THE CHIPS
1.5 kg (3 lb) potatoes, peeled
and cut

FOR THE CHILLI MIX
1 tbsp white mustard seed
1 tbsp black peppercorns
1 tbsp cumin seeds
2 tbsp paprika
1 tbsp chilli powder
1 tbsp oregano
2 tbsp thyme
1 tbsp salt

TO ADD
2 garlic cloves
1 onion

Do something a little different with
chips, by adding a Cajun taste from
Louisiana. These are ideal as a snack or
as a side dish.

METHOD
1. Peel and cut the potatoes for the
   chips – either deep-fry or sauté
   in oil.
2. While the chips are cooking, make
   the chilli mix. Gently heat the
   mustard, pepper and cumin seeds
   to bring out their flavours.
3. Cool, and then add the other
   spices, herbs and salt and grind to
   a fine powder. Finely chop the
   garlic and the onion and mix with
   the powdered spices.
4. When the chips are almost cooked,
   add the chilli mix to taste.
5. Garnish with cut lemon or lime.

THAI RED CURRY PASTE

INGREDIENTS
1/2 tsp coriander seeds
1/2 tsp caraway seeds
5 cloves
5 black peppercorns
1/4 tsp grated nutmeg
5 large red chillies, de-seeded
    and chopped
3 cloves of garlic
1 small red onion, chopped
2.5 cm (1 in.) fresh ginger root
1 stalk lemon grass chopped
rind of 1 lemon
2 tbsp chopped fresh coriander
1 tsp salt
2 tbsp vegetable oil or peanut oil

Use this easy-to-make paste – enough for two meals – fresh with fish or chicken for an authentic curry flavour.

METHOD
1. Grind the seeds, cloves and peppercorns.
2. Mix with the other ingredients to a rough paste in a food processor.
3. Use the paste immediately or store in an airtight container in the fridge.

> **TIP**
> MAKE A GREEN CURRY PASTE BY USING GREEN CHILLIES AND A WHITE ONION.

TIP

GREEN MASALA PASTE CAN
BE USED WITH FISH OR
CHICKEN. MARINATE THE CHICKEN
OR FISH WITH CHILLI
(IF PREFERRED), LEMON JUICE AND
OIL, THEN FRY WITH
ONION IN A PAN.
ADD THE MASALA PASTE,
COVER AND COOK THROUGH.

INDIAN GREEN MASALA

INGREDIENTS
6 cardamom pods
3 cloves
1 tbsp turmeric
salt
3 garlic cloves
1/2 tbsp fenugreek seeds (soaked
    overnight in water)
2.5 cm (1 in.) piece of
    root ginger, grated
25 g (1 oz) chopped mint
25 g (1 oz) chopped coriander
I green pepper, de-seeded and
    chopped
28 ml (1 fl oz) white cider vinegar
56 ml (2 fl oz) sesame oil

This mild, minty masala paste can be
used with fish or chicken or added to
lentil dishes such as dhal. There's
enough here for one or two meals.

METHOD
1. Heat the cardamom and cloves
   gently in a pan. Cool and grind
   them with the turmeric and a
   little salt.
2. Blend the rest of the ingredients
   into a purée.
3. Heat the oil, then add the paste.
   When it bubbles take off the heat.
4. Use immediately or allow to cool
   and store in an airtight jar in
   the fridge.

INDIAN TARKA DHAL

INGREDIENTS
FOR THE LENTIL DHAL

250 g (8 oz) red lentils
1.4 l (2¹/₂ pints) water
250 g (8 oz) tin chopped tomatoes
3 red chillies, finely chopped
¹/₂ tsp ground turmeric
2.5 cm (1 in.) piece of ginger root, grated
2 tbsp tamarind paste
2 tbsp soft brown sugar
2 tsp salt

FOR THE TARKA

2 tbsp oil
1 small cinnamon stick
4 cloves
¹/₂ tbsp black mustard seed
¹/₄ tsp cumin seeds
¹/₄ tsp fenugreek seeds

This simple lentil dish has a delicious, authentic Indian taste and is cheap and quick to make. Tarka is an Indian method for bringing out the flavour of spices by cooking them in hot oil. There is enough here to serve four.

METHOD

1. For the dhal, rinse the lentils, then put them with the water in a heavy iron pan, and bring to the boil.
2. Simmer for around 25 minutes until the lentils are cooked and soft. Add the tinned tomatoes, chillies, turmeric, ginger, tamarind paste, sugar and salt. Allow to simmer.
3. For the tarka, heat the oil in a small pan.

4. Allow the oil to smoke, then add the spices, and stir over a low heat for about a minute.
5. Remove the cinnamon stick and the cloves before adding the tarka to the lentil dhal.
6. Serve with chopped coriander, rice and chutney.

TIP

THE RECIPE FOR CHAI VARIES ACROSS INDIA, AND OFTEN EACH FAMILY WILL HAVE THEIR OWN FAVOURITE METHOD OF PREPARATION. IN THE SAME WAY YOU CAN EXPERIMENT WITH TASTES AND QUANTITY TO MAKE YOUR OWN CHAI. VANILLA, NUTMEG AND LIQUORICE ARE OTHER SPICES OFTEN USED.

CHAI

INGREDIENTS
2 cloves
1 cardamom pod
small cinnamon stick
350 ml (12 fl oz) water
small piece fresh root ginger
pinch of ground black pepper
$1/4$ cup whole milk
1 tbsp unrefined cane sugar
1 tbsp black tea such
    as Assam

Chai – which is spiced milk tea – is the national drink of India. Sometimes sold commercially as tea latte, it is a delicious spicy drink. The quantity made here will serve two.

METHOD
1. Crush the cloves, cardamom and cinnamon, and put them in a saucepan.
2. Add the water, ginger and pepper, and bring to the boil.
3. Allow to brew for five minutes.
4. Add the milk and sugar, and bring to the boil once more.
5. Take off the heat, and add the black tea.
6. Brew for three minutes or to taste.
7. Strain and serve in warm glasses.

MULLED WINE

INGREDIENTS
1 stick cinnamon
9 cloves
2.5 cm (1 in.) piece root ginger,
    bruised
1 tsp grated nutmeg
3 tbsp unrefined cane sugar
1 sliced orange
1 bottle red wine
120 ml (4 fl oz) brandy

This warmed, aromatic drink is
ideal for fireside evenings and
winter parties.

METHOD
1. Put the dry ingredients in a heavy
   saucepan, and pour in the wine
   and brandy.
2. Heat gently, but do not boil.
3. Allow time for the spices
   to infuse.
4. Serve warm in glasses.

TIP
USE THIS RECIPE AS A BASE AND
ADD, OR EXCLUDE, INGREDIENTS
TO TASTE. THERE IS NO SET WAY
TO MULL WINE – THE ROMANS
ADDED HONEY, MYRRH, AND
PEPPER, AS WELL AS INGREDIENTS
SUCH AS DATE STONES, SAFFRON
AND EVEN WORMWOOD.

RUM PUNCH

INGREDIENTS
1 l (33 fl oz) cider
2 cinnamon sticks
10 allspice berries
250 ml (8 fl oz) lemon juice
1 tbsp soft cane sugar,
    or to taste
750 ml (25 fl oz) dark rum
grated nutmeg to sprinkle on top

Rum punch works well as a spicy sundown party drink. These quantities will serve ten.

METHOD
1. Heat the cider with the cinnamon, allspice, lemon juice and sugar and brew for about 30 minutes but do not boil.
2. Add the rum and serve in glasses with a sprinkling of grated nutmeg.

TIP
YOU CAN USE CLOVES AND NUTMEG IN PLACE OF ALLSPICE, AND WATER IN PLACE OF CIDER.

CONCLUSION

THE LUXURY AND NECESSITY OF SPICES

For thousands of years aromatic substances known as spices arrived unheralded in the markets and ports of distant cultures. Sold as extraordinary and exotic luxuries, they soon made themselves indispensable.

Sugar, chocolate, chilli, vanilla, nutmeg and cinnamon were all introduced as strange delights but now these spices are so much part of our lives that they are regarded as necessities. The simple fact is that the more one uses spices, the more one needs them.